There's America's Lost treasure Uncovered inside Odyssey of Hidden Wealth Book :

The Quest for Timeless Riches Discovering America's Lost Wealth

By

Joe Carson – Brown

Contents

Introduction: The Call to Adventure

Somewhere in the vast and diverse landscapes of the United States, a treasure worth millions of dollars lies hidden, waiting to be discovered. This is not a myth or a legend—it is real, tangible, and ready for those with the curiosity, determination, and adventurous spirit to find it. This book, *There's Treasure Inside*, is your map, your guide, and your first step into the greatest treasure hunt in American history.

I am Jon Collins-Black, a lifelong collector, historian, and seeker of the extraordinary. Over decades, I have curated a treasure trove filled with items that span the realms of history, culture, and wealth. This treasure is not just about monetary value, though its worth is undeniable. It is a collection designed to inspire, provoke curiosity, and challenge individuals to see the world—and themselves—in a new light.

The idea of hiding this treasure came to me as a way to give something back to the world, to create a legacy of adventure and discovery. I wanted to craft an experience that would ignite a sense of wonder and exploration in people, much like the great stories of treasure hunters and explorers I've admired since childhood. This is not merely a game; it is a journey, both physical and intellectual, that can change your life in profound ways.

What Awaits You?

The treasure contains an eclectic mix of items, each chosen to appeal to a wide range of interests and passions. Among the riches are:

- **Modern treasures** like Bitcoin and gold.

- **Timeless artifacts** from history, including relics tied to figures like Pablo Picasso, George Washington, and Jackie Onassis.

- **Rare collectibles** such as Pokémon cards, sports memorabilia, and gems from the original Forrest Fenn treasure.

- **Cultural and artistic treasures** like rare gems and shipwreck artifacts.

Each piece carries its own story, its own piece of history, and its own significance, making the hunt as much about uncovering narratives as it is about finding valuables.

A Journey Beyond Treasure

While the allure of finding millions of dollars in riches may draw you in, this book and the journey it invites you to take are about much more than wealth. At its core, *There's Treasure Inside* is about exploration—of the world, of history, and of yourself. The hunt will challenge your resourcefulness, sharpen your critical thinking, and encourage you to connect with places and stories you might never have encountered otherwise.

In the pages that follow, you'll find everything you need to get started. From the details of the treasure itself to the rules of the hunt, from maps and clues to personal anecdotes and historical insights, this book is your guide to a journey unlike any other.

Why This Treasure Hunt Matters

In an age dominated by screens and virtual experiences, this treasure hunt is a call to step outside, to explore the real world, and to connect with its rich tapestry of landscapes, history, and culture. It's a chance to be part of something larger than yourself, to contribute to a story that will echo for generations to come.

Whether you aim to claim the treasure or simply enjoy the thrill of the search, *There's Treasure Inside* invites you to become part of a legacy. Are you ready to accept the challenge?

Turn the page, and let the adventure begin.

Chapter 1: What's Inside the Treasure?

When you imagine treasure, what comes to mind? Is it chests overflowing with gold coins, glittering gemstones, or priceless relics from the past? The treasure hidden within the United States is all that—and more. It's a curated collection of items, each chosen for its unique value, story, and appeal. This chapter dives into the contents of the treasure, giving you a glimpse into what's waiting for you to discover.

1.1 Modern Wealth: Bitcoin and Gold

In today's world, wealth has taken on new forms. Digital currencies like Bitcoin represent the cutting edge of finance and technology. Included in the treasure are secure wallets containing Bitcoin, offering a piece of the future to whoever finds it.

Alongside this modern asset are classic symbols of wealth: gold coins, bullion, and rare minted pieces. These timeless treasures hold their value regardless of the era and remain a tangible connection to the world's most enduring form of currency.

1.2 Historical Artifacts and Shipwreck Bounty

For the history enthusiast, the treasure includes relics from the past that tell incredible stories. Among these are:

- **Artifacts linked to American history**, such as Revolutionary War-era tools and Civil War relics.

- **Shipwreck treasures**, including coins, jewelry, and artifacts recovered from underwater expeditions. These pieces carry the mystique of journeys cut short and fortunes lost to the sea.

Each item in this category is more than an object—it's a time machine, offering a glimpse into the lives of those who came before us.

1.3 Rare Collectibles: Pokémon Cards and Sports Memorabilia

For collectors and enthusiasts, the treasure offers something truly exciting: rare and valuable items from pop culture and sports history. Highlights include:

- **First-edition Pokémon cards**, including the iconic Charizard card, beloved by fans worldwide.

- **Autographed sports memorabilia**, featuring jerseys, balls, and equipment signed by legends like Michael Jordan, Serena Williams, and Tom Brady.

These collectibles represent the passions and achievements of our time, making them priceless to the right finder.

1.4 Precious Gems and Rare Metals

Nothing captures the imagination like the sparkle of a diamond or the deep hue of an emerald. The treasure contains a variety of gemstones, including:

- Diamonds, sapphires, rubies, and emeralds, cut and uncut.

- Precious metals like platinum and silver in intricate designs or raw form.

These items are not only valuable but beautiful, offering a sense of timeless elegance.

1.5 The Legacy of the Forrest Fenn Treasure

Among the treasure are artifacts from the famous Forrest Fenn hunt, a legendary quest that captivated adventurers worldwide.

These pieces carry a legacy of adventure and mystery, tying this hunt to one of the most iconic treasure stories of our time.

By including these artifacts, the treasure pays homage to the spirit of exploration and discovery that defined Fenn's legacy.

1.6 Cultural and Historical Icons

Some items in the treasure have belonged to or been created by figures who shaped history and culture. Examples include:

- **An art piece attributed to Pablo Picasso**, embodying the creative genius of the 20th century.

- **A personal item of George Washington**, a connection to the nation's founding father.

- **Jewelry once owned by Jackie Onassis**, symbolizing timeless grace and sophistication.

Each of these items carries a story of its own, offering not just monetary value but a deep connection to moments and people who changed the world.

1.7 Why This Treasure is Unique

Unlike traditional treasures focused solely on gold or gems, this collection is designed to reflect the diversity of human achievement, creativity, and ambition. From cutting-edge Bitcoin to artifacts steeped in history, every item was selected to inspire and excite a wide range of treasure hunters.

This treasure is not just about wealth; it's about curiosity, discovery, and the thrill of the hunt. It is designed to challenge seekers to think, explore, and connect with both the physical world and the stories it holds.

1.8 What Will You Find?

Ultimately, the treasure is a mirror for the seeker. For some, it will represent financial freedom. For others, it will be the stories and artifacts that capture their imagination. No matter what drives you, the hunt is yours to shape, and the treasure is yours to claim.

As you turn the pages of this book and embark on your journey, remember: the treasure inside is only as great as the adventure it inspires. Will you be the one to uncover it?

Chapter 2: The Makers of History

Every treasure has a story, and some of the most compelling stories come from the people and events that shaped the world. The treasure hidden in this hunt includes artifacts and items linked to historical figures whose lives and legacies changed the course of history. This chapter dives into the creators, owners, and inspirations behind these priceless treasures, offering a deeper connection to the past.

2.1 Pablo Picasso: The Genius of Modern Art

Among the treasure is an artwork attributed to Pablo Picasso, one of the most influential artists of the 20th century. Picasso's bold, boundary-breaking style redefined what art could be, and his works remain highly sought after.

This piece is more than a painting—it's a symbol of creativity, rebellion, and innovation. For the finder, it represents a direct link to an artist whose influence can still be felt in modern culture.

2.2 George Washington: The Nation's Founding Father

A personal item linked to George Washington, America's first president, is also part of the treasure. Washington's leadership during the Revolutionary War and his presidency shaped the foundation of the United States.

This artifact—a relic of Washington's daily life—offers a tangible connection to the man behind the history. Whether it's a letter, a tool, or an object he carried, this item embodies the courage and vision of a leader who helped build a nation.

2.3 Jackie Onassis: A Style Icon and Cultural Figure

Known for her elegance, intelligence, and strength, Jackie Kennedy Onassis captured the world's imagination during her time as First Lady and beyond. The treasure includes a piece of jewelry or personal accessory once owned by Jackie, reflecting her timeless sophistication.

This item is more than a beautiful object—it's a symbol of resilience and grace under pressure, qualities Jackie demonstrated during some of the most tumultuous moments in American history.

2.4 Amelia Earhart: The Pioneer of the Skies

Amelia Earhart broke barriers as an aviator and a woman, becoming a symbol of courage and determination. Included in the treasure is an artifact tied to Earhart—perhaps a map, a tool she used, or memorabilia connected to her groundbreaking flights.

This relic serves as a reminder of her fearless spirit and her contributions to aviation and gender equality.

2.5 Andrew Carnegie: The Titan of Industry

A piece tied to Andrew Carnegie, one of the richest men in history and a great philanthropist, is also part of the collection. Carnegie's legacy includes the rise of the steel industry and his commitment to funding libraries, education, and the arts.

The artifact—a document, a coin, or a personal effect—represents the dual nature of Carnegie's life: a relentless pursuit of success balanced by a deep belief in giving back to society.

2.6 Henry David Thoreau: The Philosopher of Simplicity

Henry David Thoreau's writings on nature, civil disobedience, and self-reliance have inspired generations. The treasure includes an item linked to Thoreau—perhaps a first-edition book, a personal object, or a manuscript fragment.

This piece represents Thoreau's commitment to living deliberately and finding meaning in the simple, profound moments of life.

2.7 Louis Comfort Tiffany: The Master of Art Nouveau

Tiffany's name is synonymous with beauty and craftsmanship. The treasure includes a Tiffany creation—possibly a piece of jewelry, a lamp, or decorative art. Known for his innovation in glassmaking and design, Tiffany's work remains a benchmark of artistic excellence.

This artifact is a celebration of creativity and a reminder of the enduring power of beauty in everyday life.

2.8 What These Figures Represent

Each artifact in the treasure isn't just a physical object—it's a bridge to a larger story. These items reflect the values, struggles, and achievements of their original creators or owners. They serve as reminders of the human capacity for greatness, resilience, and innovation.

By including these historical and cultural artifacts, the treasure transforms from a collection of valuables into a collection of legacies. Each piece carries a story, and finding it means becoming a part of that story.

2.9 Why These Items Matter to the Hunt

The inclusion of these artifacts adds depth to the treasure hunt. They provide not only a financial incentive but also a meaningful connection to history. Finding an item linked to Picasso or Earhart isn't just a discovery—it's a moment of connection with the past.

As you continue reading this book and deciphering the clues, keep in mind that this treasure is more than material wealth. It's an opportunity to engage with history, uncover stories, and become part of a legacy that transcends time.

Chapter 3: How to Use This Book as Your Treasure Map

Embarking on the greatest treasure hunt in American history is no small feat, but with the right guidance, tools, and mindset, it's entirely possible. This chapter serves as your ultimate guide to using *There's Treasure Inside* effectively as your map and compass. From decoding the clues to planning your search, these pages will arm you with the knowledge and strategies needed to take the first steps on your journey.

3.1 Understanding the Structure of the Book

This book is more than a collection of stories and information—it's a carefully designed map to lead you to the treasure. Each chapter contains:

- **Clues**: Hidden within the text, illustrations, and chapter titles are hints that will guide you closer to the treasure's location.

- **Historical and Cultural Context**: Understanding the significance of the treasure pieces can help you decode certain clues.

- **Practical Tips**: Advice on tools, techniques, and strategies you'll need for a successful search.

Think of each page as a puzzle piece. Together, they create the full picture you'll need to find the treasure.

3.2 Decoding the Clues

The clues in this book come in various forms, including:

- **Textual Clues**: Subtle hints embedded in the narrative, often disguised as historical or cultural facts.

- **Visual Clues**: Maps, symbols, and diagrams that may point to specific locations.

- **Hidden Codes**: Ciphers, anagrams, and numerical sequences that require decoding to reveal their meaning.

Pro Tip: Pay attention to details. A seemingly insignificant piece of information might be a vital clue when connected to others.

3.3 Planning Your Search

Once you've gathered clues, it's time to strategize. Treasure hunting isn't just about luck; it's about preparation and persistence.

- **Start with Research**: Use the information in this book to narrow down possible regions or landmarks. Cross-reference clues with historical data, maps, and local lore.

- **Map Your Route**: Identify key locations based on the clues you've deciphered. A well-planned journey will save you time and effort.

- **Prepare for the Terrain**: Whether you're heading to a dense forest, a remote desert, or a historic urban area, make sure you're equipped for the environment.

3.4 Essential Tools and Resources

No treasure hunter sets out unprepared. Here's a list of tools and resources to bring on your adventure:

- **Maps and GPS Devices**: For navigation and pinpointing specific locations.

- **Metal Detector**: Useful for uncovering buried items.

- **Notebook and Camera**: To document findings and revisit details.

- **Research Materials**: Books, online archives, and historical records related to the clues.

- **Survival Gear**: Depending on the terrain, pack essentials like food, water, first-aid kits, and weather-appropriate clothing.

Digital Resources: Consider apps and websites for decoding ciphers, identifying landmarks, and tracking your progress.

3.5 Teamwork vs. Solo Adventures

Treasure hunting can be a deeply personal journey or a collaborative effort. Each approach has its advantages:

- **Solo Hunts**: Offer complete independence and the thrill of personal discovery.

- **Team Efforts**: Bring diverse skills and perspectives to the hunt, making it easier to decode complex clues and cover more ground.

If working in a team, establish clear roles and responsibilities to avoid misunderstandings. Communication is key.

3.6 Staying Safe and Legal

The thrill of the hunt should never come at the cost of safety or legality. Keep these tips in mind:

- **Obtain Permissions**: If your search takes you onto private property or protected lands, seek appropriate permissions first.

- **Know the Laws**: Be aware of regulations regarding treasure hunting, metal detecting, and artifact collection in your area.

- **Stay Safe**: Avoid risky behaviors like climbing unsafe structures or venturing into hazardous environments unprepared.

Pro Tip: Use the resources in this book's appendices for guidance on legal and safety considerations.

3.7 Tracking Your Progress

Documenting your journey is crucial, both for keeping track of clues and for sharing your story if you succeed. Keep a record of:

- Clues you've deciphered.

- Locations you've searched.

- Observations and discoveries along the way.

A clear record can help you refine your strategy and ensure you don't miss vital connections between clues.

3.8 What to Expect on the Hunt

Treasure hunting is as much about the journey as it is about the prize. Along the way, you can expect:

- **Moments of Frustration**: Not every clue will be easy to solve, and not every lead will pay off. Persistence is key.

- **Personal Growth**: The challenges you face will teach you resilience, creativity, and problem-solving skills.

- **Unexpected Discoveries**: Even if you don't find the treasure immediately, you're likely to uncover fascinating stories, places, and people along the way.

3.9 Your First Step

Now that you know how to use this book, it's time to take the first step. Begin by reading through the entire book, noting anything that stands out as a potential clue. Create a plan based on what resonates with you, and get ready to embark on an adventure that could change your life.

Remember, treasure hunting is about more than just the prize—it's about the journey, the stories you uncover, and the memories you create. You have the map, the tools, and the spirit. Now, it's time to start the hunt.

Chapter 4: Decoding the Clues – The Art of Puzzle Solving

Finding the hidden treasure isn't just about looking in the right places—it's about understanding the clues that point to those places. Chapter 4 is your guide to unraveling the intricate puzzles woven into *There's Treasure Inside*. Each clue has been carefully crafted to challenge your mind, expand your perspective, and lead you one step closer to the ultimate prize.

4.1 The Language of Clues

Clues are not always straightforward. They might come in forms that require interpretation, deduction, and creative thinking. In this book, clues can manifest as:

- **Riddles**: Playful or poetic puzzles that hint at locations or concepts.

- **Anagrams and Wordplay**: Scrambled letters or phrases that, when decoded, reveal hidden meanings.

- **Historical References**: Hints buried in stories or facts about historical events, places, or figures.

- **Visuals**: Maps, illustrations, or diagrams with subtle markers or symbols.

Each type of clue demands a different skill set, so being versatile in your approach is crucial.

4.2 The Power of Observation

Decoding clues begins with observation. Sometimes, the most critical hint lies in plain sight but can only be recognized by those paying attention.

- **Look for Patterns**: Repeated words, numbers, or symbols might be more than coincidence.

- **Examine Every Detail**: Even the smallest elements, like punctuation or capitalization, might carry meaning.

- **Consider the Context**: A clue's surroundings—both within the book and in real-world locations—can provide vital insights.

Pro Tip: Take your time. Rushing through a clue might cause you to overlook its most important details.

4.3 Tools for Decoding Clues

You don't need to be a professional cryptographer to solve these puzzles, but having the right tools and techniques can make all the difference:

- **Cipher Decoders**: Learn the basics of common ciphers like Caesar, Vigenère, and substitution codes. Online tools can also assist with complex encryptions.

- **Map Skills**: Some clues may involve coordinates, topographical features, or landmarks. Understanding maps is essential.

- **Word and Phrase Analyzers**: Tools like Scrabble helpers or anagram solvers can help decode jumbled letters or phrases.

- **Historical Resources**: Access to encyclopedias, archives, and historical maps can provide context to clues linked to the past.

Pro Tip: Keep a decoding kit—a notebook, pens, a compass, and access to digital resources—for quick and efficient problem-solving.

4.4 Step-by-Step Guide to Solving Clues

1. **Read the Clue Carefully**: Identify the type of clue—riddle, code, visual—and break it down into smaller, manageable parts.

2. **Search for Keywords**: Highlight words or phrases that seem unusual or significant.

3. **Analyze Symbols and Numbers**: Look for recurring symbols, patterns, or numerical sequences.

4. **Cross-Reference**: Use the information in the book and external resources to find connections.

5. **Test Hypotheses**: Don't hesitate to try multiple interpretations until something fits.

Example: If a clue says, "Where the water meets the sun," you might consider coastal locations, rivers, or lakes at sunrise. The phrase could also hint at a specific landmark named after water or the sun.

4.5 The Role of Creativity

Logic and research are vital, but creativity is often the key to cracking a complex clue. Sometimes, the answer lies outside the box.

- **Think Metaphorically**: A clue like "a window to the past" could refer to a historical site, a museum, or even an artifact like a photograph.

- **Embrace Ambiguity**: Many clues are intentionally open to multiple interpretations. Explore all possibilities before narrowing down.

- **Collaborate**: Sharing ideas with others can spark new perspectives and solutions.

4.6 Practicing with Sample Clues

To help you hone your skills, here are some practice clues similar to what you'll encounter in the treasure hunt:

1. **Riddle**:

   I stand tall where battles were fought, my shadow marks the hour.

   - Possible Answer: A monument or historical site with a sundial, such as a battlefield memorial.

2. **Anagram**:

   "SHE WALTZES TO NOON"

   - Solution: Rearrange the letters to spell *"Stonewall South"*—possibly referring to a location in the southern United States.

3. **Visual-Clue**:

A map with an "X" marked at a seemingly random spot might require cross-referencing with historical events or geological features to decode its meaning.

4.7 Mistakes to Avoid

Even seasoned treasure hunters can fall into common traps. Here's what to watch out for:

- **Overthinking**: Sometimes, the simplest explanation is the correct one.

- **Ignoring Context**: A clue taken out of context can lead you astray.

- **Tunnel Vision**: Don't fixate on a single interpretation—be open to reevaluating your approach.

Pro Tip: Keep track of all your attempts, even the incorrect ones. They might provide insights later.

4.8 The Rewards of Puzzle Solving

Decoding clues is about more than finding the treasure. It's an intellectual adventure that sharpens your mind, enhances your problem-solving skills, and teaches you to see the world from new perspectives. Each clue solved is a small victory, a step closer to the ultimate goal.

Chapter 5: The Search Begins – Planning and Executing Your Hunt

With your clues decoded and your treasure map in hand, it's time to take action. Chapter 5 will guide you through the crucial steps of planning and executing your treasure hunt. From preparing your team and tools to managing your time and resources, this chapter will ensure that you approach the search with strategy, determination, and confidence.

5.1 Understanding the Terrain

Before embarking on your hunt, it's essential to understand the lay of the land. Each treasure has its unique location, which may range from bustling cities to remote wilderness areas. Whether you're exploring a historical site or venturing into the wilderness, understanding the terrain is vital to your success.

- **Study the Geography**: Research the area where you believe the treasure may be hidden. Use topographical maps, satellite imagery, and any other resources to familiarize yourself with the region's features.

- **Climate and Weather**: Pay close attention to weather patterns. Certain locations may be difficult or dangerous to explore during particular seasons. Check seasonal weather forecasts and pack accordingly.

- **Local History and Culture**: Learn about the local history, myths, and traditions. Many clues are connected to specific historical events, and understanding the local lore can provide valuable insight.

5.2 Assembling Your Team

Treasure hunting can be a solitary pursuit, but it's often more successful when done as part of a team. Whether you choose to hunt alone or with others, you'll need to assess your strengths, weaknesses, and resources to form the ideal team for the task.

- **The Leader**: This person coordinates the hunt, interprets clues, and makes final decisions. They should have good leadership skills, be decisive, and have a thorough understanding of the book's clues.

- **The Researcher**: A team member who excels at finding information, whether online or in physical archives. They can help uncover historical references and background information on specific locations.

- **The Navigator**: Someone skilled in reading maps and using GPS tools. This person will chart the route, helping the team avoid getting lost and ensuring the group stays on track.

- **The Scout/Explorer**: A member who enjoys physically navigating the environment—whether hiking, exploring ruins, or visiting historical sites. They should be fit and comfortable in the outdoors.

- **The Historian/Expert**: An expert in the history, culture, or field related to the treasure. This person can provide insights into obscure references or specific historical periods.

The right mix of personalities and skills is crucial. However, even if you are working alone, developing these skills yourself can increase your chances of success.

5.3 Choosing the Right Tools

No treasure hunt is complete without the proper tools. Whether you're searching for a hidden artifact in a city, digging for buried treasure, or exploring caves, your tools will determine how effectively and efficiently you can carry out your search.

- **Essential Gear:**

  - **Compass and Maps**: Old-fashioned tools like a compass and topographical maps are still incredibly useful, even in the digital age.

  - **Metal Detectors**: If you suspect there may be buried treasure, a quality metal detector is a must-have.

  - **Multitools and Shovels**: Digging and uncovering treasures will require sturdy tools. A good multitool and digging equipment like spades or trowels are essential.

  - **Safety Gear**: Make sure to pack safety equipment such as first-aid kits, water bottles, and weather-appropriate clothing. You should also carry a flashlight for nighttime searches.

- **Recording Equipment**: Cameras, notebooks, and voice recorders will help document your findings, ideas, and thoughts along the way.

- **Tech Tools**:

  - **GPS Devices**: A reliable GPS tool is crucial for marking coordinates and mapping out areas.

  - **Smartphones and Apps**: Many apps are available to help you analyze images, decode ciphers, and store information.

  - **Drones**: For aerial surveys of large areas, a drone can help capture crucial imagery.

5.4 Planning Your Route

With your team and tools ready, it's time to plan your route. A well-thought-out route can save you valuable time and energy.

- **Break It Down**: Start by reviewing your clues and narrowing down the potential locations based on their proximity to one another.

- **Prioritize Locations**: Some locations may seem more likely to hold treasure than others. Prioritize these areas, but be open to exploring other leads.

- **Create a Timeline**: Map out the route, determine how long it will take to travel, and establish a realistic timeline. Factor in rest breaks, research periods, and time for unexpected delays.

- **Reevaluate Often**: As you gather more information during the hunt, continue to reassess your strategy. Be prepared to change your route or approach if new clues emerge.

5.5 Navigating the Search Area

Once you arrive at your destination, your skills as a navigator and your ability to interpret clues on-site will become crucial. The search is more than just following a path—it's about observing your surroundings, testing hypotheses, and adapting to new information.

- **Start with the Obvious**: Begin your search at the most logical locations based on your clues. For example, if a clue points to an old oak tree by a river, that's a natural starting point.

- **Search Methodically**: Don't rush the process. Take time to carefully inspect every location. Use systematic methods to survey large areas, breaking them down into smaller sections for thorough searches.

- **Consider All Possibilities**: If your initial search doesn't yield results, reconsider your interpretation of the clue. Look for overlooked details or alternative meanings.

5.6 Dealing with Challenges and Obstacles

Treasure hunting is rarely smooth sailing. Along the way, you'll encounter obstacles that challenge your physical, mental, and emotional limits.

- **Weather**: Sudden storms, extreme heat, or cold can affect your search. Always have backup plans and shelter options.

- **Difficult Terrain**: Some treasures may be hidden in places that are hard to reach—mountain cliffs, dense forests, or underwater locations. Be prepared for physical challenges.

- **Legal and Safety Issues**: Ensure that you're hunting on land where you have permission. Also, make sure you're aware of local laws regarding metal detecting, artifact collecting, and excavation.

- **Frustration**: The hunt may take longer than you expect, or you might hit a dead end. Stay persistent and keep your morale high by focusing on the joy of discovery.

5.7 Tracking Your Progress and Adjusting Your Plan

As you progress, regularly document everything you find, even if it seems insignificant. Keeping track of your clues, locations, and discoveries is essential for piecing together the bigger picture.

- **Review Your Findings**: After each day of searching, sit down with your team (or by yourself) and go over what you've discovered.

- **Reassess Your Approach**: If things aren't adding up, it may be time to rethink your strategy. Was a clue misunderstood? Could there be a different interpretation of the evidence?

- **Celebrate Small Wins**: Every breakthrough, even a small one, is a victory. Celebrate progress to keep the momentum going.

Chapter 6: The Treasure Unveiled – Discovering the Hidden Wealth

After all the preparation, clue decoding, planning, and journeying, you've finally reached the moment of truth: discovering the treasure. Chapter 6 explores the final steps of the treasure hunt, from finding the treasure itself to understanding its significance and claiming your reward. But it's not just about the tangible riches—you'll also explore the deeper, personal treasures that emerge from the process.

6.1 The Final Clue – A Moment of Clarity

As you approach the final leg of your journey, everything you've done so far culminates in one crucial moment: the unveiling of the final clue. This is where everything you've learned, every decision, and every strategy comes into play. But finding the treasure is often not a straightforward process.

- **Trust the Process**: The final clue might not reveal itself immediately. Sometimes, it takes stepping back and seeing the puzzle from a new perspective. Stay calm, trust your instincts, and reanalyze all the information you've gathered.

- **Revisit the Clues**: Go over your earlier clues and the places you've already searched. A minor detail you missed earlier could be the key to solving the puzzle.

- **Stay Focused**: As you approach the location or object that might hold the treasure, maintain your focus. Excitement can cloud your judgment, so be methodical in your approach.

Pro Tip: Sometimes, the treasure isn't in the first place you expect. Go back to the last clue you cracked and review the path again. Look for alternative interpretations of the location or symbol.

6.2 The Moment of Discovery – What You'll Feel

There's nothing quite like the moment when you first realize that you've uncovered the treasure. Whether you've found a hidden vault of gold coins, an antique artifact, or a rare gem, the emotions that accompany this moment will be profound.

- **Shock and Awe**: The initial discovery might come as a shock, as it's often hard to believe that you've succeeded after such a long search. This is the moment when reality sets in—you're holding something of immense value.

- **Joy and Euphoria**: The joy of discovery is both personal and shared. You may feel elated as the hours, days, or even years of work culminate in the moment when the treasure is found.

- **Gratitude and Fulfillment**: In addition to the thrill, there's a deep sense of gratitude—toward your team, your resources, and your dedication. The journey was just as valuable as the discovery itself.

Pro Tip: Record the moment. Whether through a photo, video, or journal entry, capturing this feeling can help you reflect on the journey long after the treasure has been claimed.

6.3 Examining the Treasure – What's Inside?

When you finally lay your hands on the treasure, it's time to thoroughly inspect and appreciate what you've found. The treasure you've uncovered will be as unique as the hunt itself. It could include:

- **Precious Metals and Gems**: Gold, silver, and rare gems like diamonds, sapphires, and emeralds are often highly sought-after treasures.

- **Historical Artifacts**: Items like ancient coins, swords, letters, or manuscripts carry historical significance and could be worth far more than their material value.

- **Rare Collectibles**: Trading cards, vintage toys, or pieces of memorabilia from significant events may also be part of the treasure. Items once owned by figures like George Washington, Amelia Earhart, or Picasso may tell a story beyond their price tag.

- **Cryptocurrency and Modern Wealth**: In keeping with the changing times, part of the treasure could be in digital form, like Bitcoin, NFTs, or digital art.

Inspecting each piece carefully and researching its provenance can help determine its true value. You may want to seek an expert's opinion, especially when dealing with valuable or rare items.

6.4 The Significance of the Treasure

While the treasure itself has tangible value, its true significance lies in the deeper lessons it imparts. Treasure hunting isn't just about finding wealth—it's about the transformation that occurs along the way.

- **Historical Significance**: Many of the treasures you uncover may have historical importance. For instance, discovering an artifact that once belonged to a significant historical figure or civilization could deepen your understanding of history and humanity.

- **Personal Growth**: The pursuit of treasure challenges you in ways that go beyond physical and mental limits. It teaches resilience, patience, critical thinking, and the importance of persistence.

- **Connection to the Past**: The treasure you uncover may serve as a bridge to a time long gone, helping you connect with people and events that shaped history. Understanding the stories behind the objects makes the discovery all the more meaningful.

- **Exploration of Self**: Beyond the material wealth, treasure hunting is also a journey of self-discovery. The skills you've developed, the lessons you've learned, and the people you've met along the way are treasures in themselves.

Pro Tip: Consider what your treasure means beyond its value. How has the journey impacted you personally? What has it taught you about your own character and capabilities?

6.5 Claiming the Treasure – What's Next?

Once the treasure is found, the next step is to claim it. Depending on where and how the treasure was hidden, this might involve the following steps:

- **Legal Considerations**: Depending on the treasure's location, there may be legal considerations regarding ownership, especially if it's on public or private land. Make sure you understand the laws related to treasure hunting and artifact ownership in the region.

- **Valuation**: Consult with experts to determine the true market value of your findings. Appraisers, auction houses, or museums can offer insight into the worth of rare items and artifacts.

- **Documentation**: Document the treasure thoroughly—photographs, videos, and a written account of the discovery process can help protect your claims and provide future reference.

- **Preservation and Care**: Some treasures, especially historical artifacts, may need to be properly cared for to ensure their longevity. Whether it's a piece of artwork or an ancient relic, learn how to preserve and protect your finds.

6.6 Sharing the Treasure – A Legacy of Discovery

What you choose to do with your newfound wealth or artifacts is up to you, but many treasure hunters choose to share their discoveries in some way. Whether you keep it for personal enjoyment or decide to share it with the world, the legacy of the treasure can live on:

- **Share with the Public**: Some treasures are best shared with the world. Donating significant historical finds to museums or archives ensures their preservation and allows others to appreciate them.

- **Legacy of Discovery**: If your hunt has led to groundbreaking discoveries or rare items, consider sharing your story. Writing about your journey, whether in the form of a book, documentary, or article, can inspire future generations of treasure hunters.

- **Philanthropy**: Some choose to sell their treasures and donate the proceeds to causes they care about, leaving a legacy of giving and support for others.

Pro Tip: If you decide to keep your treasure, remember to protect it. Store valuable items in a secure location, and consider the insurance and long-term care they may require.

6.7 The Deeper Treasure – Lessons Learned

As the treasure hunt ends, the deeper treasures emerge—the personal growth, the knowledge gained, the skills honed, and the relationships formed along the way. The true treasure often lies in the journey, not the destination.

- **The Value of Perseverance**: The obstacles you overcame, the challenges you faced, and the lessons you learned are priceless. They've shaped you into a more resilient, knowledgeable, and self-aware individual.

- **The Power of Collaboration**: If you worked as part of a team, the bonds you formed with fellow treasure hunters will be some of the most valuable treasures you have. Trust, communication, and shared experiences create lasting relationships.

- **A New Perspective on Life**: The hunt may have changed the way you look at the world. The excitement of discovery, the joy of exploration, and the satisfaction of success can inspire you to continue seeking new adventures in every aspect of life.

Chapter 7: The Legacy of Treasure – Beyond the Hunt

The treasure hunt may have ended, but the journey doesn't stop there. In this chapter, we will explore the profound legacy that treasure hunting can leave behind, not just in terms of material wealth, but also in the impact it has on your life and the world around you. The treasures you uncover, both tangible and intangible, will carry on influencing future generations, inspiring others to embark on their own quests for discovery, and leaving behind a legacy that transcends time.

7.1 The Ripple Effect – Inspiring Future Generations

One of the most powerful aspects of treasure hunting is its ability to inspire others. As you've discovered, the journey is filled with not just physical challenges, but intellectual and emotional ones that push you to grow and evolve. Your story can become a beacon of inspiration for future adventurers.

- **Passing Down Knowledge**: As you reflect on the clues you deciphered, the places you explored, and the historical context of the treasures you unearthed, you realize that treasure hunting is about more than finding wealth—it's about learning. Sharing your knowledge with others, especially the younger generation, ensures that the legacy of discovery lives on.

- **Cultivating Curiosity**: The hunt for treasure can spark a curiosity that drives people to seek answers to questions they may not have considered before. You've set an example of what it means to embrace the unknown and search for something bigger than yourself.

- **Fostering a Spirit of Adventure**: There is something inherently adventurous about the act of treasure hunting.

Your journey has demonstrated that adventure isn't just for the movies—it's something anyone can embark upon. By telling your story, you encourage others to take on their own adventures, whether literal or metaphorical.

Pro Tip: Share your journey with others. Whether through blogs, podcasts, books, or speaking engagements, recounting your experience can spark curiosity and excitement in those who follow in your footsteps.

7.2 The Power of Storytelling – The Treasure of Narratives

As much as treasure hunting is about the discovery of physical wealth, it is also about the stories that accompany the hunt. These stories carry emotional value, cultural significance, and historical depth, creating a rich narrative that endures long after the treasure has been claimed.

- **Weaving a Tapestry of History**: Each treasure you find is linked to a larger story—whether it's a historical artifact, a relic of a past civilization, or a memento from an influential person. These items connect the present with the past, and they become a bridge to understanding the stories that shaped our world.

- **Personal Narratives**: Your personal journey through the hunt is a story in itself. The challenges you overcame, the discoveries you made, and the insights you gained are part of a larger narrative that others can learn from.

- **Cultural Significance**: Some treasures have cultural implications that are much larger than their monetary value. An artifact from a long-lost civilization, or a piece of memorabilia from a groundbreaking event, can spark discussions about cultural heritage, preservation, and identity. These items can inspire societal reflection and dialogue.

Pro Tip: Keep a journal of your treasure hunting experiences. Recording your thoughts, emotions, and the discoveries you make along the way can preserve the richness of your narrative for future generations.

7.3 Sharing the Wealth – How to Use Your Treasure for Good

While the material wealth found in a treasure hunt is often thrilling, the true power lies in how that wealth can be used for the betterment of society. The treasures you've uncovered—whether they're rare artifacts, gold, or modern assets like cryptocurrency—carry the potential to make a profound impact.

- **Philanthropy and Giving Back**: If you find that your treasure is of significant value, consider using it for charitable causes. Donating a portion of the wealth to support education, healthcare, or the arts can create lasting benefits. Many treasure hunters choose to support organizations that align with their values and passions.

- **Preserving History**: Some of the treasures you find may have historical importance. By donating or loaning these items to museums or cultural institutions, you ensure their preservation for future generations.

- **Creating Opportunities**: Your newfound wealth can be used to create opportunities for others. You might fund educational scholarships, create grants for emerging artists, or invest in local community projects.

- **Support Conservation Efforts**: Many treasures are related to nature or historical landscapes. If your treasure hunt has uncovered items tied to the environment or endangered ecosystems, use the proceeds to support conservation efforts and the protection of natural resources.

Pro Tip: Consider setting up a charitable foundation or partnering with existing ones to ensure that your wealth is being used in a meaningful and impactful way.

7.4 Leaving a Lasting Legacy – What Will You Leave Behind?

The legacy of a treasure hunt isn't just about the wealth you leave behind; it's about the impact you have on the world and the stories you create. What you leave behind will carry far more weight than material possessions. This is your opportunity to think about the future and how your discoveries will be remembered.

- **Mentorship and Guidance**: As someone who has completed a successful treasure hunt, you can offer mentorship and guidance to others looking to undertake similar journeys. By passing on your knowledge and experiences, you ensure that the hunt for treasure continues.

- **A Monument to Discovery**: You might choose to create a physical monument—a park, a statue, or a foundation—in honor of your journey. This could be a place where future generations can come to reflect on the value of exploration, adventure, and discovery.

- **A Written Legacy**: Writing a book, creating documentaries, or recording your journey in other forms allows you to document and share your experience. By doing so, you ensure that your legacy will live on and inspire others to embark on their own quests.

Pro Tip: Think about how your discovery can inspire people in the future. Whether through an artifact, a story, or a community initiative, make sure that the legacy of your hunt is part of your enduring impact on the world.

7.5 The Treasure Within – Self-Discovery and Personal Growth

While the physical treasure you've uncovered is undoubtedly valuable, the true treasure often lies in the personal growth that happens along the journey. The treasure hunt teaches you lessons about who you are, how you react to challenges, and how you can adapt and evolve.

- **The Discovery of Resilience**: Through the highs and lows of the hunt, you discover how resilient you truly are. The moments of doubt, frustration, and failure are just as important as the moments of success. They shape your character and build inner strength.

- **The Power of Patience**: Treasure hunting teaches you that patience is an invaluable trait. The search may take longer than you anticipate, and the clues might not always be clear. But it's in these moments of waiting that you learn to trust the process and believe in yourself.

- **Building Confidence**: As you overcome obstacles, solve complex puzzles, and inch closer to the treasure, you build confidence in your abilities. You learn to trust your instincts, make decisions under pressure, and move forward even in uncertainty.

- **Understanding the Bigger Picture**: Through the treasure hunt, you gain a new perspective on life. The value of the treasure becomes less about wealth and more about the deeper lessons you've learned along the way.

Pro Tip: Reflect on your personal growth. Take time to understand how the journey has shaped you and how the lessons you've learned will continue to influence your life moving forward.

Chapter 8: The Art of the Hunt – Mastering the Skills of a Treasure Seeker

Treasure hunting is not merely about luck; it's about the art of seeking and the mastery of various skills that combine intellect, creativity, and persistence. In this chapter, we delve into the essential skills needed to be a successful treasure hunter, including research, critical thinking, perseverance, and the ability to interpret clues. These skills are the foundation upon which every great treasure hunt is built, and they will serve you well as you embark on your journey to uncover the greatest treasures waiting to be found.

8.1 Research: The Foundation of Every Treasure Hunt

Before setting foot in the field, treasure hunters must first master the art of research. Whether it's reading historical accounts, studying maps, or reviewing documents related to the treasure's origin, the ability to gather and analyze information is crucial.

- **Historical Context**: Understanding the historical significance of the treasure will help you recognize the context in which it was hidden. Investigate the history of the location, the people involved, and the events surrounding the treasure. Knowing who hid the treasure and why they did it will provide invaluable insights into its likely location.

- **Studying Maps**: Maps are one of the most valuable tools in a treasure hunter's arsenal. Old maps, topographical maps, nautical charts, and satellite imagery can all reveal hidden clues that are invisible to the naked eye. Knowing how to read and analyze maps can often make the difference between success and failure.

- **Consulting Experts**: Often, the path to treasure is obscured by centuries of misinformation or legends. Seeking advice from historians, archaeologists, and experts in the field can offer new perspectives. These individuals can help you interpret clues, understand historical contexts, and avoid common pitfalls.

Pro Tip: Build a solid research plan before embarking on your hunt. Gather as much information as possible from diverse sources, and use it to construct a theory about the treasure's location and its history.

8.2 Critical Thinking and Problem Solving – Decoding the Clues

As you begin your treasure hunt, you'll encounter clues that are intentionally cryptic or obscure. To decipher these hidden messages, you'll need strong critical thinking and problem-solving skills. Each clue is a puzzle that, when pieced together, reveals the next step of your journey.

- **Logical Deduction**: Often, clues will point to multiple possible answers. Using logical deduction, you must eliminate the unlikely possibilities to focus on the most plausible explanations. Ask yourself questions like: "What could this clue be referring to in historical terms?" or "How does this clue relate to the environment I'm exploring?"

- **Pattern Recognition**: Many treasures are hidden based on patterns, whether they are geographical, numerical, or linguistic. Developing the ability to spot patterns in the clues you discover will enable you to make better decisions and move forward in your search.

- **Creative Thinking**: Not all clues are straightforward. Some may require a leap of imagination or unconventional thinking. This might include interpreting cryptic poetry, deciphering symbols, or considering abstract connections between seemingly unrelated pieces of information.

- **The Power of Persistence**: Often, the most difficult clues take the longest to solve. It's in these moments of frustration that persistence becomes key. Take breaks when needed, but don't give up. The treasure won't reveal itself without effort and tenacity.

Pro Tip: Keep a notebook or digital log of all the clues you find. This will help you identify connections and ensure you don't overlook any potential leads.

8.3 Tools of the Trade – Equipment and Technology for Treasure Seekers

Modern technology has revolutionized the way treasure hunters conduct their searches. While many traditional tools are still essential, the right equipment can significantly increase your chances of success.

- **Metal Detectors**: One of the most popular tools for treasure hunters, metal detectors help locate hidden artifacts and treasures beneath the ground. Different detectors have varying levels of sensitivity, so choosing the right model for the type of terrain you'll be working in is critical.

- **Drones and Aerial Surveys**: Drones have become invaluable tools in treasure hunting, especially for those searching in large or difficult-to-reach areas. Drones can be used to capture aerial imagery, which can then be analyzed to reveal hidden landscapes, structures, or unusual patterns.

- **Geophysical Tools**: Ground-penetrating radar (GPR) and magnetometers are used by more advanced treasure hunters and archaeologists to detect buried objects. These tools provide a detailed image of the subsurface, allowing treasure hunters to pinpoint specific locations where objects may be buried.

- **Compasses, GPS, and Satellite Mapping**: Navigational tools are essential for any treasure hunt. A compass and GPS device can help you maintain your bearings, while satellite mapping technology can give you a bird's-eye view of the area you're exploring.

- **Traditional Tools**: Simple tools like shovels, trowels, pickaxes, and brushes are still necessary for excavating sites once you've pinpointed where the treasure is located. The care you take with these tools can mean the difference between preserving an artifact and damaging it beyond recognition.

Pro Tip: Understand the limitations of the tools you use. No single tool will provide all the answers, so it's important to use a combination of methods and technology to gather information.

8.4 Navigating Challenges – Overcoming Obstacles and Staying Focused

No treasure hunt is without its challenges. Whether it's dealing with difficult terrain, interpreting misleading clues, or facing emotional and mental fatigue, the path to treasure is rarely smooth. Understanding how to navigate these obstacles will help you stay focused and motivated, even when the hunt becomes difficult.

- **Physical Challenges**: Some treasure hunts take place in remote or harsh environments, such as dense forests, deserts, or underwater. Prepare yourself physically by training for the type of environment you will be working in, and always be prepared with the proper clothing and equipment.

- **Dealing with Setbacks**: Not every clue will lead to immediate success. Many treasure hunts involve dead ends, false leads, and setbacks. Learning to deal with disappointment and refocus your efforts will help you persevere when the hunt becomes frustrating.

- **Emotional Resilience**: The treasure hunt will test your emotional endurance. At times, you may feel isolated, discouraged, or overwhelmed. It's important to stay positive and remind yourself why you embarked on this journey in the first place. Mental resilience is just as important as physical stamina.

- **Staying Focused**: As your hunt progresses, distractions and temptations can lead you astray. The key to success lies in your ability to stay focused on your ultimate goal.

Avoid jumping to conclusions or getting sidetracked by exciting but irrelevant leads. Trust in your research, stay methodical, and keep your eyes on the prize.

Pro Tip: Maintain a treasure hunter's mindset. View each challenge as an opportunity to learn and grow. Celebrate small wins, and remember that persistence is often the key to unlocking big rewards.

8.5 The Role of Intuition – Trusting Your Gut in the Hunt

While treasure hunting involves logic and careful planning, intuition often plays a crucial role in guiding your decisions. Many successful treasure hunters will tell you that their greatest discoveries came not from maps or research but from a feeling in their gut that told them they were on the right track.

- **Recognizing the Right Moment**: Sometimes, the treasure reveals itself when you least expect it. Trust your intuition when it tells you to pause, reconsider a clue, or approach a search area from a different angle.

- **The Feeling of "Being Close"**: As you get closer to the treasure, you may experience a sense of knowing. This could be the result of your brain subconsciously connecting the dots between your research and physical environment.

- **Balancing Logic and Intuition**: The best treasure hunters are those who can strike a balance between analytical thinking and intuition. The key is not to rely solely on one over the other but to use both in harmony.

Pro Tip: When you feel uncertain, take a moment to step back and listen to your instincts. Sometimes, the treasure hunt requires a leap of faith—trust that your inner voice is guiding you in the right direction.

Chapter 9: The Pursuit of Legacy – The Treasure That Lasts Beyond Wealth

In the world of treasure hunting, many are drawn by the promise of riches—gold coins, rare gems, priceless artifacts, and the thrill of unearthing something that others have longed for. But as you dig deeper into the heart of treasure seeking, you'll find that the true treasure isn't just the material wealth you uncover. It's the legacy you leave behind, the stories you create, and the lessons you learn. This chapter focuses on the broader, often more rewarding, pursuit of legacy—the treasure that lasts beyond wealth and has the power to shape the future.

9.1 The True Value of Treasure

While many treasure hunts promise riches beyond imagination, the reality is that material wealth can be fleeting. Whether it's a collection of coins, valuable artifacts, or precious metals, these items can lose their value over time, especially when they fall into the wrong hands or lose their historical context.

However, the legacy of the treasure—the impact it has on your life, the lives of others, and the story it tells—can have an eternal significance. The true treasure is not the wealth itself, but the journey it allows you to undertake and the lessons you gain along the way.

- **The Emotional and Psychological Impact**: The pursuit of treasure is a deeply personal journey. Along the way, you will face challenges, disappointments, moments of doubt, and unexpected triumphs. These experiences shape you, change you, and build the resilience needed to achieve your goals. The value of these life lessons cannot be measured in dollars and cents.

- **The Story of Discovery**: Every treasure has a story— whether it's the history of the people who hid it, the clues left behind, or the challenges overcome to find it. When you uncover treasure, you're not just finding wealth; you're unlocking a piece of history. The story you create along the way—how you discovered the treasure, what it meant to you, and how it changes your life—becomes the legacy that endures long after the treasure itself is spent.

Pro Tip: Remember that the journey to the treasure is just as important as the treasure itself. Celebrate the personal growth and experiences that shape your path to discovery.

9.2 Creating a Legacy – What You Leave Behind

When treasure hunters strike it rich, they often face a dilemma—what to do with their newfound wealth. While some may choose to hoard their riches or live a life of luxury, others find that sharing their wealth and knowledge creates a legacy that lasts for generations.

Creating a lasting legacy is not just about money—it's about impact. What will your treasure mean to those who come after you? How will your discoveries inspire future generations of treasure hunters, historians, and adventurers?

- **Philanthropy and Giving Back**: Many successful treasure hunters choose to share their wealth with those in need, either through charitable donations, establishing scholarships, or funding projects that benefit communities. Giving back not only transforms lives but also creates a legacy of generosity and goodwill that resonates long after the treasure has been spent.

- **Preserving History**: Treasures often come with rich histories, and preserving these stories is crucial to understanding their significance. Many treasure hunters donate their findings to museums, universities, or public archives, ensuring that the treasure's story is told for years to come. By doing so, you are contributing to the cultural fabric of humanity and ensuring that the knowledge and beauty of your discovery are passed down to future generations.

- **Educating Others**: Knowledge is a powerful treasure. By sharing your skills, insights, and experiences with others, you help cultivate a new generation of treasure seekers. Whether through mentoring, writing books, or teaching at schools and institutions, the knowledge you share will leave an indelible mark on the future of treasure hunting.

Pro Tip: Consider how your discoveries and wealth can serve others. Creating a legacy of knowledge, generosity, and preservation can be far more valuable than any material treasure.

9.3 The Ripple Effect – The Influence of Your Actions

The choices you make as a treasure hunter will ripple outward, affecting not only your own life but also the lives of others. The treasure you seek and uncover often has the power to create a wave of influence, inspiring others to pursue their own dreams, tackle their own challenges, and believe in their own potential.

- **Inspiring Others**: As your story unfolds, you may inspire others to embark on their own quests for knowledge, wealth, and adventure. Your journey—filled with ups and downs, failures, and triumphs—can motivate others to face challenges with courage and resilience.

- **Building Community**: Many treasure hunts require collaboration—working with fellow seekers, historians, archaeologists, and experts. These collaborations create communities of like-minded individuals, all working toward a common goal. By building relationships and fostering teamwork, you create a lasting network of people who can support one another and keep the spirit of treasure hunting alive.

- **Changing Perspectives**: Sometimes, finding treasure doesn't just change your life—it changes the way others view the world. Treasure hunting can alter people's perspectives on history, human achievement, and the pursuit of dreams. By unlocking a treasure, you have the opportunity to change how people think about the world, reminding them of the possibilities that lie beyond the everyday.

Pro Tip: Recognize that your actions will affect others in ways you may not anticipate. Your journey can inspire and empower people far beyond your immediate circle.

9.4 Timeless Treasures – The Treasure of Self-Discovery

While uncovering material wealth is often the goal of treasure hunters, one of the most profound treasures you can find is the treasure within yourself. Treasure hunting is an act of self-discovery. As you face challenges, push beyond your limits, and learn new skills, you'll uncover hidden parts of yourself. These are the treasures that cannot be quantified but are far more valuable than anything material.

- **Building Confidence**: Treasure hunting requires belief in your abilities. As you unlock clues, overcome obstacles, and inch closer to your goal, you build a sense of accomplishment and self-worth that carries over into every area of your life.

- **Facing Fear and Doubt**: The hunt often involves moments of uncertainty—fear of failure, fear of the unknown, fear of loss. Confronting these fears head-on and pushing through doubt is one of the greatest treasures you can gain from the pursuit.

- **Gaining Knowledge**: The process of treasure hunting involves continual learning. From understanding history and geography to mastering tools and techniques, every step you take brings new knowledge. The more you learn, the more capable and empowered you become.

- **Discovering Your Passion**: For many treasure hunters, the search is not just about the treasure itself—it's about finding a passion that drives them. The excitement of the hunt, the thrill of discovery, and the satisfaction of solving puzzles become an integral part of who you are.

Pro Tip: Remember that the journey of treasure hunting is as much about personal growth as it is about discovery. Embrace the process, and treasure the lessons learned along the way.

9.5 A Legacy of Stories – Sharing Your Journey with the World

One of the most lasting elements of treasure hunting is the stories that arise from it. Whether you find the treasure or not, your journey creates a narrative—a personal adventure that can inspire others, educate future generations, and entertain millions.

- **Telling Your Story**: Whether you write a book, make a documentary, or simply share your experience with friends and family, telling the story of your treasure hunt ensures that your journey lives on. The narrative of your quest, the ups and downs, and the lessons learned can inspire others to take on their own adventures.

- **Documenting the Experience**: Many treasure hunters keep journals or logbooks to document every step of their journey. This detailed record not only serves as a personal memoir but can also be an invaluable resource for future treasure seekers.

- **Passing Down the Tales**: Treasure hunting often becomes a tradition. Parents pass down their love for the hunt to their children, who carry the stories into the future. In this way, treasure hunts become part of a family or cultural legacy, preserving the adventures and lessons for generations.

Pro Tip: Share your treasure hunting story, not just for fame or glory, but to inspire others to believe in their own potential and to remind them that the greatest treasures often lie in the journey itself.

Chapter 10: The Treasure Inside You – Uncovering the Riches of Self-Belief

As we conclude our journey through the physical and material treasures hidden throughout the world, we must pause and reflect on the ultimate treasure that lies within each of us. It's easy to get caught up in the allure of gold, rare artifacts, and historical riches. But the greatest treasure of all is not something that can be found in the ground or within ancient maps—it is the treasure within ourselves. This chapter is dedicated to understanding how the greatest treasure is already inside of you, waiting to be uncovered through self-belief, purpose, and action.

10.1 The Power of Self-Belief – Your Inner Treasure

The first and most important step in finding the treasure within yourself is recognizing that you already possess everything you need to achieve greatness. Self-belief is the cornerstone of any treasure hunt, not just the external ones, but those that happen in the realms of the mind and spirit.

- **Trusting Your Potential**: Every human being is born with unique talents, abilities, and potential. But many of us fail to recognize this potential because we've been conditioned to doubt ourselves or compare ourselves to others. When you truly believe in your abilities, you unlock the first door to discovering your inner treasure.

- **Overcoming Doubt and Fear**: Self-doubt is often the greatest barrier to success. The voice of uncertainty whispers in our minds, telling us that we are not capable, that our dreams are too big, or that failure is inevitable. But every great treasure hunter, every great achiever, faces these doubts. The difference lies in their ability to push past them, to continue forward despite the fear. Self-belief enables you to silence that voice of doubt and stay focused on the treasure that lies ahead.

- **The Role of Resilience**: No treasure hunt is ever smooth sailing. There will be setbacks, detours, and challenges. But the key to success is resilience—the ability to bounce back, learn from failure, and keep pushing toward your goal. Cultivating self-belief empowers you to persist, no matter the difficulties that arise.

Pro Tip: The first step to finding the treasure within is shifting your mindset from one of self-doubt to one of possibility. Embrace the idea that you are capable of achieving your dreams, and watch how that belief unlocks new potential in you.

10.2 Living with Purpose – Navigating Your Own Treasure Map

Purpose is the compass that guides you on your journey, both in treasure hunting and in life. Without purpose, you wander aimlessly, never truly discovering your inner wealth. When you live with purpose, you create a treasure map for your life—a path that helps you focus on what truly matters and helps you stay motivated during difficult times.

- **Defining Your Purpose**: Understanding your purpose is key to unlocking your potential. What drives you? What are you passionate about? What legacy do you want to leave behind? These questions are the foundation for uncovering your inner treasure. When you have a clear sense of purpose, your actions align with your values, and your journey becomes meaningful.

- **Staying True to Your Vision**: Life is full of distractions, and the path to discovering your inner treasure may not always be clear. But staying true to your vision means ignoring the noise around you and focusing on what matters most. It means taking the time to define your goals and building a strategy to achieve them, regardless of the obstacles you may face.

- **Finding Meaning in Everyday Actions**: Purpose doesn't just come from big, life-altering decisions. Often, the treasure is found in the small, everyday actions that align with your values. Whether it's helping others, pursuing a hobby, or creating something meaningful, every action you take with purpose brings you closer to the treasure that lies within.

Pro Tip: Reflect on your values and passions to clarify your purpose. When you live with purpose, you transform ordinary actions into stepping stones toward uncovering your true potential.

10.3 Embracing Change – The Transformation of the Treasure Hunter

As you embark on the treasure hunt of self-discovery, one of the most important realizations is that you are constantly changing. Personal growth is a journey that requires flexibility, adaptability, and a willingness to evolve. Just as you must learn to adapt to new clues and challenges in a traditional treasure hunt, you must also learn to navigate the shifting landscapes of your own life.

- **The Journey of Transformation**: Personal transformation doesn't happen overnight. It's a gradual process that occurs as you challenge yourself, learn from experiences, and open yourself up to new possibilities. The treasure inside you is revealed through your growth and evolution.

- **Embracing New Perspectives**: To uncover the treasure within, you must be willing to change your perspective. Sometimes, we hold onto outdated beliefs about who we are or what we're capable of. The treasure hunter's mindset is one of constant learning and adaptability. It's about embracing new ideas and being open to change.

- **Building New Habits**: Transformation often comes down to the habits you form. Whether it's waking up earlier, meditating, exercising, or developing new skills, your habits shape the person you are becoming. Positive habits create momentum and move you closer to discovering the treasure within.

Pro Tip: Personal transformation is not a destination, but a lifelong journey. Embrace the process of change, and know that every step you take brings you closer to revealing the wealth of potential inside you.

10.4 The Treasure of Mindset – Shaping Your Reality

The way you think shapes the way you experience the world. Your mindset is one of the most powerful tools you can use to uncover your inner treasure. A positive, growth-oriented mindset empowers you to overcome challenges, attract opportunities, and achieve your goals.

- **The Growth Mindset**: A growth mindset is the belief that you can develop your abilities through dedication and hard work. It's the understanding that intelligence, talent, and success are not fixed traits, but can be cultivated with effort. Embracing this mindset opens the door to endless possibilities and encourages you to take risks, learn from mistakes, and keep growing.

- **Visualizing Success**: Visualization is a powerful technique that can help you unlock your potential. By picturing your success and imagining the person you want to become, you align your thoughts and actions with your desires. The more you visualize the treasure inside you, the more likely you are to manifest it in your life.

- **Affirmations and Positive Thinking**: The words you speak to yourself shape your reality. By practicing daily affirmations and focusing on positive thoughts, you begin to rewire your brain for success. This mindset shift is essential for unlocking your true potential and creating the life you desire.

Pro Tip: Cultivate a growth mindset by challenging your negative thoughts and replacing them with empowering beliefs. The treasure inside you is waiting to be revealed through the power of positive thinking.

10.5 The Treasure of Connection – Building Relationships that Enrich Your Life

No treasure hunt is ever truly solitary. To uncover the wealth within yourself, you need the support of others. The people you surround yourself with—friends, mentors, family, and even acquaintances—play a vital role in your journey. Relationships are the treasures that enrich your life and help you grow.

- **The Power of Mentorship**: Seeking guidance from others who have walked the path before you can be invaluable. A mentor can provide insight, offer support, and help you navigate the challenges you face. Just as treasure hunters work with experts to decode maps and clues, you can benefit from the wisdom of those who have experienced the journey before you.

- **Creating a Supportive Network**: Surrounding yourself with like-minded individuals who support your goals and values is crucial to success. A strong network provides encouragement, accountability, and opportunities for collaboration. The relationships you build along the way will not only help you achieve your goals but also lead to personal growth and fulfillment.

- **The Treasure of Love and Friendship**: Ultimately, the relationships you cultivate with those closest to you are among the greatest treasures of all. The love, support, and companionship you receive from friends and family enrich your journey and provide you with a sense of belonging and purpose.

Pro Tip: Nurture your relationships and seek out those who encourage your personal growth. The treasure of connection is one of the most valuable assets in your life's journey.

Conclusion: Uncovering the Greatest Treasure – You

As we conclude this journey, it becomes clear that the treasure hunt we've embarked upon is far more than a pursuit of material wealth. The treasures we've explored—the rare artifacts, the precious metals, the forgotten history—are captivating and valuable, but they serve as mere metaphors for something much greater: the treasure that lies within each of us.

Throughout this book, we've uncovered the countless external treasures hidden across the United States, but perhaps the most valuable discovery is the one that's always been inside you. You have the power to achieve greatness, to find fulfillment, and to create a life rich in purpose, connection, and self-belief. These treasures aren't locked away in caves or buried beneath mountains—they are already within you, waiting to be unearthed.

By following the map of self-discovery laid out in this book, you now have the tools to unlock your potential and embrace the journey of transformation. Whether it's developing the mindset of a treasure hunter, understanding the importance of resilience, or living with purpose, the key to your personal treasure is in your hands. Every step you take, every challenge you face, brings you closer to the realization that the richest treasure is not found in the world's rarest artifacts, but in the growth and transformation that you experience along the way.

The treasure within you is not just about success or wealth. It's about living a life full of meaning, joy, and the deep satisfaction that comes from knowing you are becoming the best version of yourself. The true wealth lies in how you embrace your journey, how you learn and grow, and how you share your discoveries with others.

Now that you've uncovered the blueprint for finding this treasure, it's time to take action. Start today. Cultivate the belief that you are worthy of the riches that life has to offer. Keep your eyes open for the opportunities that surround you. Surround yourself with people who inspire and support your dreams. And most importantly, remember that the greatest treasure is not just about what you seek, but about who you become on the journey.

The treasure is inside you. It's always been there. All it takes is the courage to begin the hunt and the determination to see it through. So, go forth and claim your riches—because the treasure you seek is waiting to be found.

Your Treasure Awaits.

Made in the USA
Las Vegas, NV
26 November 2024

12734978R00063